EARTH

by Melanie Mitchell

first step nonfiction

L Lerner Publications Company · Minneapolis

This is **Earth.**

Earth is part of our
solar system.

Our solar system has nine **planets** and the **Sun.**

Earth is the third planet
from the Sun.

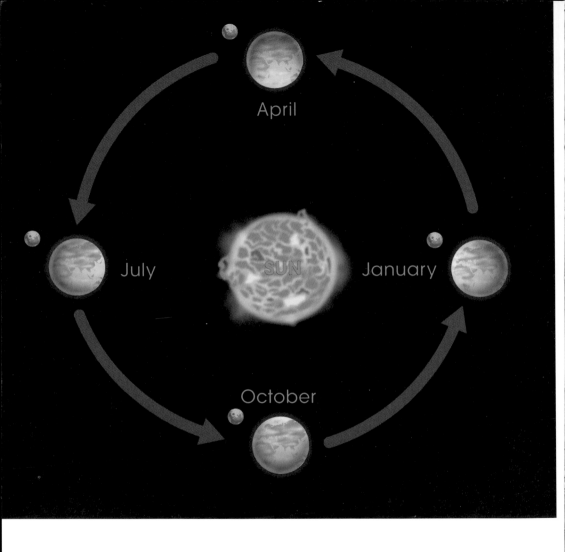

It takes Earth one year to move around the Sun.

As it moves, Earth turns
like a top.

During the day, you are
facing the Sun.

At night, Earth turns and you
are away from the Sun.

Earth gets light and heat
from the Sun.

Earth is where people,
plants, and animals live.

Earth has air for them
to **breathe.**

Earth has food for them
to eat.

Earth has water for people, plants, and animals.

Most of Earth is covered
with water.

Earth is a special planet.

We like to live on Earth!

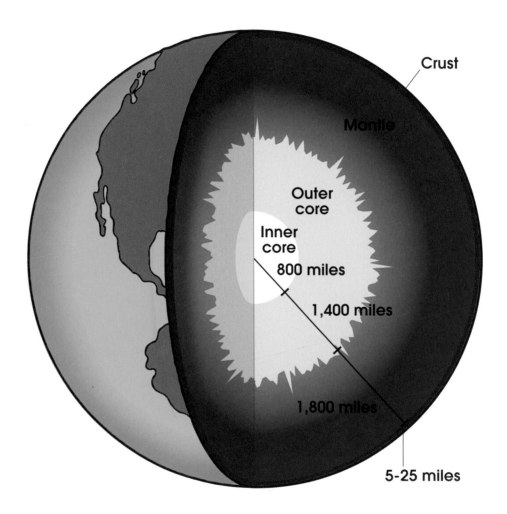

Crust

Mantle

Outer core

Inner core

800 miles

1,400 miles

1,800 miles

5-25 miles

What's inside Earth?

The inside of Earth is made out of rock and metal. The outside of Earth is called the crust. The crust is a thin layer of rock. Below the crust is a thick layer of rock. Some of the rock in this layer is very hot. This layer is called the mantle. The center of Earth is called the core. It is a ball of hot, melted metal.

Earth Fun Facts

 At least 70 percent of Earth's surface is covered by water.

 Earth travels through space at a speed of around 66,000 miles per hour.

 The coldest temperature ever recorded on Earth was 128.6 degrees Fahrenheit below zero in Antarctica.

 Earth is the fifth largest planet in our solar system.

Earth is thought to be between 4 and 5 billion years old.

 Earth is about 93 million miles from the Sun.

 The highest point on Earth is Mt. Everest at about 29,028 feet above sea level. The lowest point is in the Dead Sea at about 1,302 feet below sea level.

Glossary

 breathe – to take air into the lungs and push it out

 Earth – the planet where people live

 planets – objects that move around the Sun

 solar system – the Sun, and the planets, moons, and everything that travels around the Sun

 Sun – the star that Earth and the other planets revolve around

Index

Copyright © 2004 by Lerner Publications Company

All rights reserved. International copyright secured. No part of this book may be reproduced, stored in a retrieval system, or transmitted in any form or by any means—electronic, mechanical, photocopying, recording, or otherwise—without the prior written permission of Lerner Publications Company, except for the inclusion of brief quotations in an acknowledged review.

The photographs in this book are reproduced through the courtesy of: © Stocktrek/Corbis, front cover; © NASA, pp. 2, 3; © SuperStock, pp. 4, 22 (second from bottom); © Stone by Getty Images, pp. 5, 22 (middle); © Todd Strand/Independent Picture Service, p. 7; © Royalty-Free/Corbis, pp. 8, 22 (top); © Taxi by Getty Images, p. 9; © Rob & Ann Simpson/Photo Agora, pp. 10, 22 (bottom); © PhotoDisc Royalty-Free by Getty Images, pp. 11, 16, 22 (second from top); © National Space Science Data Center, p. 12; © Agricultural Research Service, USDA, p. 13; © Jack Milchanowski/Visuals Unlimited, p. 14; © P.I. Productions/SuperStock, p. 15; © ThinkStock/SuperStock, p. 17.

Lerner Publications Company
A division of Lerner Publishing Group
241 First Avenue North
Minneapolis, MN 55401 USA

Website address: www.lernerbooks.com

Library of Congress Cataloging-in-Publication Data

Mitchell, Melanie S.
    Earth / by Melanie Mitchell.
        p.   cm. — (First step nonfiction)
    Includes index.
    Summary: A simple introduction to the planet earth.
    ISBN: 0–8225–5137–3 (lib. bdg. : alk. paper)
    ISBN: 0–8225–3590–4 (pbk. : alk. paper)
    1. Earth—Juvenile literature. [1. Earth.] I. Title. II. Series.
QB631.4.M58 2004
550—dc21   2003005628

Manufactured in the United States of America
1 2 3 4 5 6 – DP – 09 08 07 06 05 04